SPOT

MOTORSPORTS

HOT RODS

by Alissa Thielges

amicus LEARNING

dragstrip

engine

Look for these
words and pictures
as you read.

tire

flames

Wow! What a cool car.
It is a hot rod.

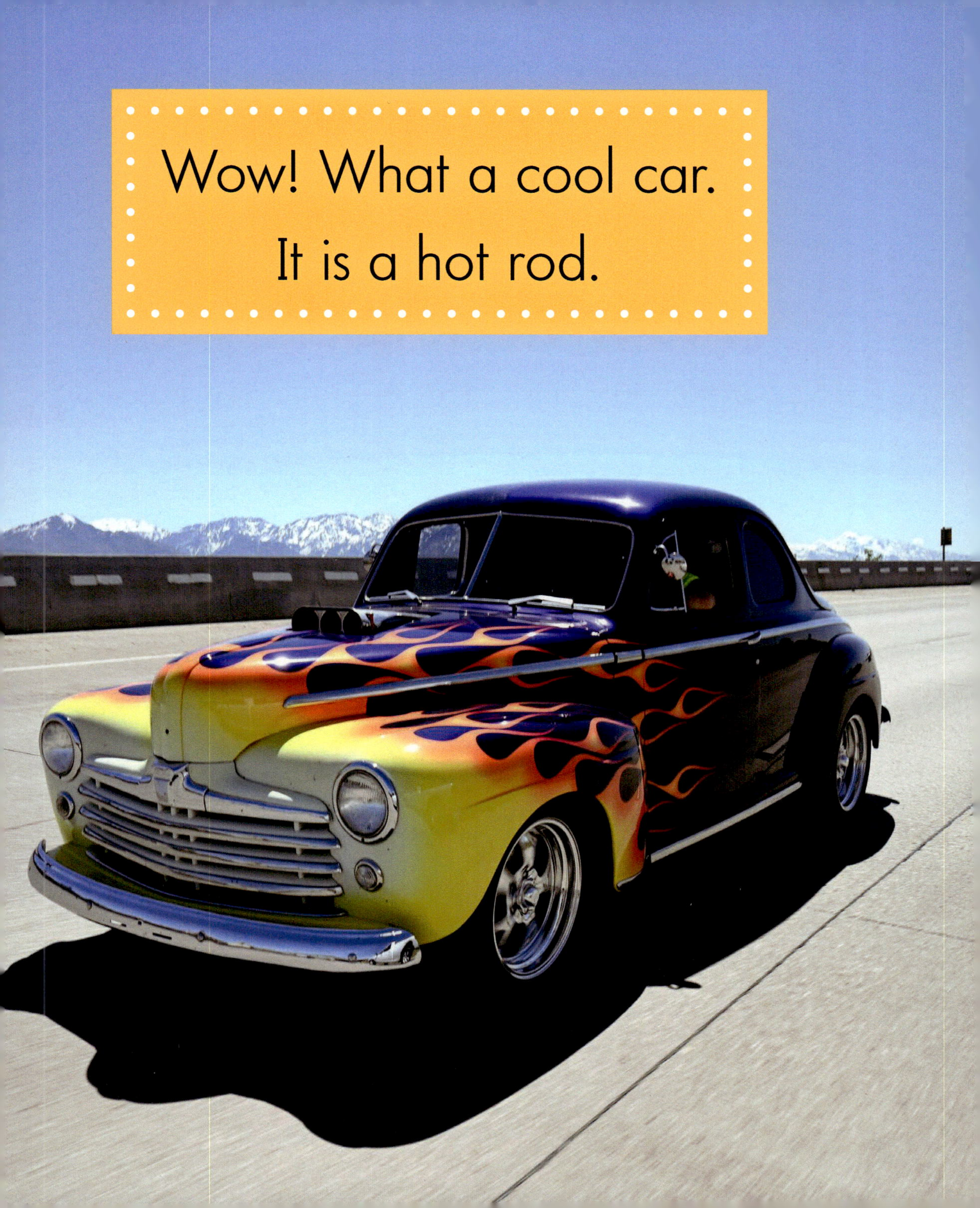

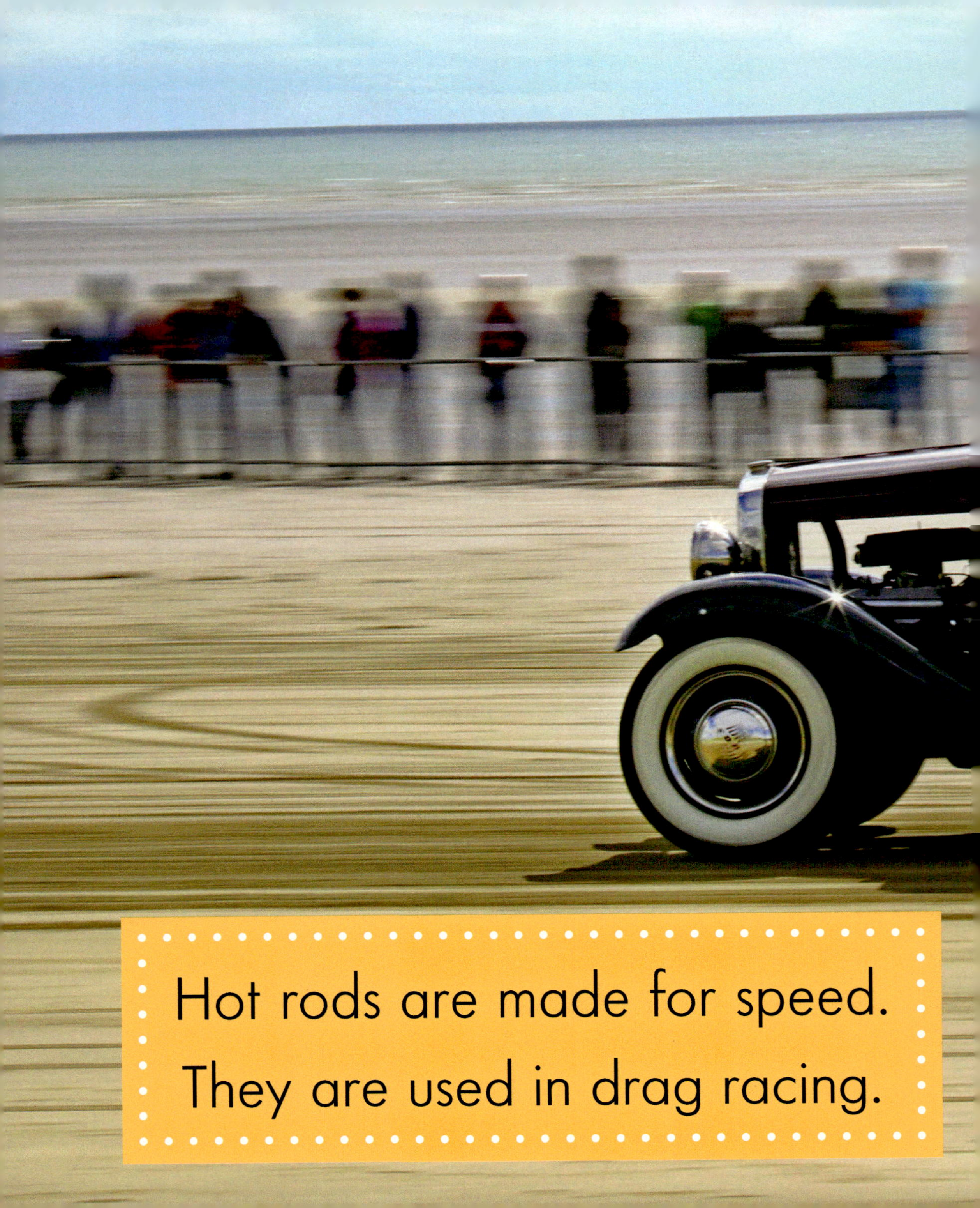

Hot rods are made for speed.
They are used in drag racing.

See the dragstrip?
It is short and straight.
Cars race on it.

dragstrip

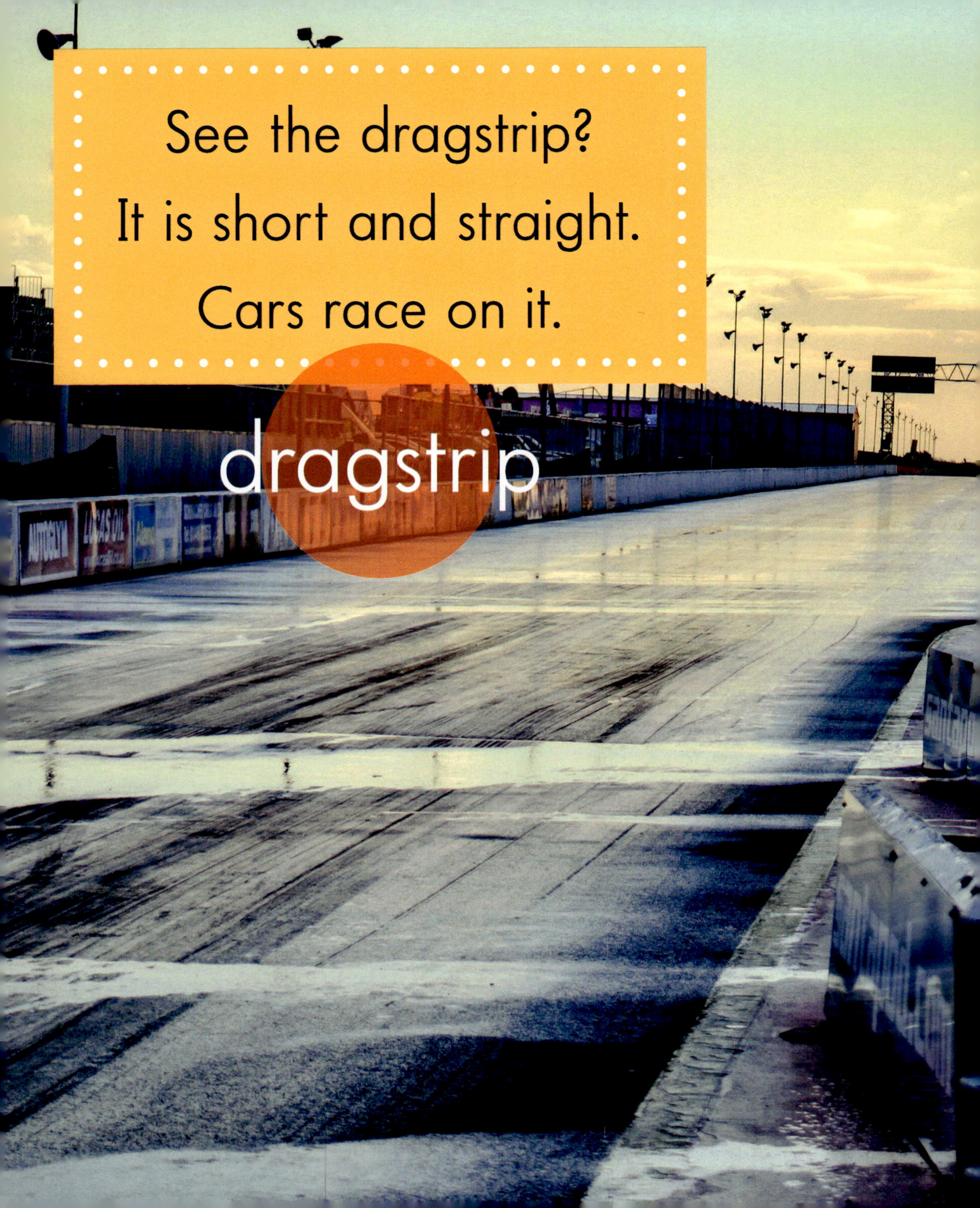

See the engine? It is big.
It gives the car top speed.

engine

Silvertown Radial

tire

See the tire?
It is wide.
It has a white stripe.

See the flames?
They are sprayed on.
The paint job makes
the car stand out.

flames

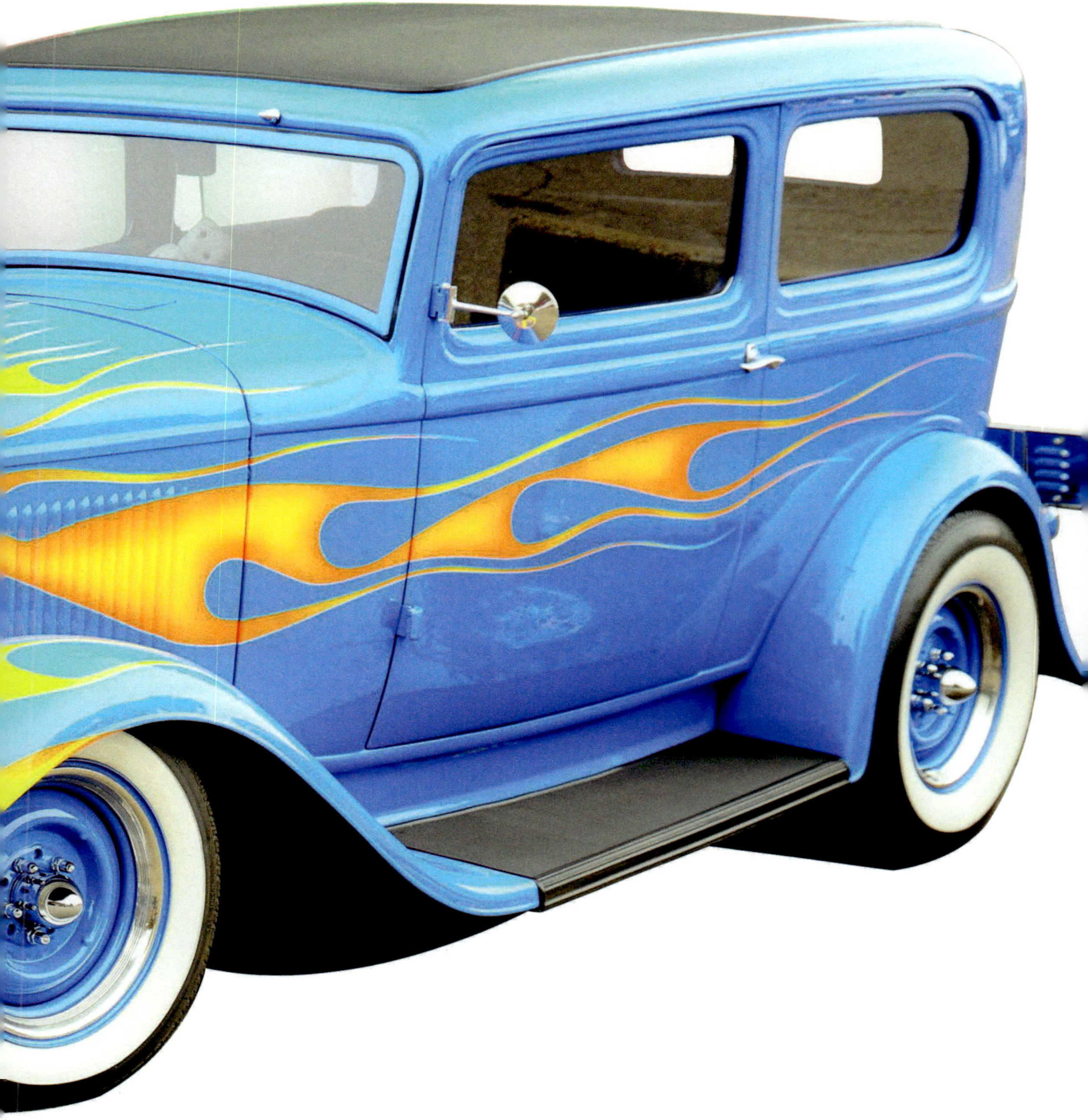

Ready to race?

Let's roll!

Did you find?

dragstrip

engine

tire

flames

SPOT

Spot is published by Amicus Learning, an imprint of Amicus
P.O. Box 227, Mankato, MN 56002
www.amicuspublishing.us

Library of Congress Cataloging-in-Publication Data
Names: Thielges, Alissa, 1995- author.
Title: Hot rods / by Alissa Thielges.
Description: Mankato, MN : Amicus Learning, [2026] | Series: Spot motorsports | Audience: Ages 4–7 | Audience: Grades K–1 | Summary: "Hot rods are fast, old-fashioned cars that are customized for car shows and drag racing. This search-and-find book reinforces new vocabulary words with simple facts and compelling photographs to teach kindergarten readers about motorsports"— Provided by publisher.
Identifiers: LCCN 2024050083 (print) | LCCN 2024050084 (ebook) | ISBN 9798892004824 (library binding) | ISBN 9798892005364 (paperback) | ISBN 9798892005906 (ebook)
Subjects: LCSH: Hot rods—Juvenile literature. | Automobiles—Customizing—Juvenile literature. | CYAC: Hot rods. | Automobiles.
Classification: LCC TL236.3 .T564 2026 (print) | LCC TL236.3 (ebook) | DDC 629.228/6—dc23/eng/20241219
LC record available at https://lccn.loc.gov/2024050083
LC ebook record available at https://lccn.loc.gov/2024050084

Ana Brauer, editor
Deb Miner, series designer
Sara Hood, book designer and photo researcher

Photos by Alamy Stock Photo/Ferenc Konya, 6–7, horst friedrichs, 4–5, Richard McDowell, 14, Robert Teed, 3; Dreamstime/Fascinating Cars, 10–11, Lynette F Gram, 1; Shutterstock/Jason Osborne, cover, Philip Pilosian, 8–9, Pichit Kaewbutta, 12–13